THE 1950s
DECADE IN PHOTOS
"THE AMERICAN DECADE"

Jim Corrigan

Enslow Publishers, Inc.
40 Industrial Road
Box 398
Berkeley Heights, NJ 07922
USA

http://www.enslow.com

Library of Congress Cataloging-in-Publication Data

Corrigan, Jim.
  The 1950s decade in photos : "the American decade" / by Jim Corrigan.
    p. cm. — (Amazing decades in photos)
  Includes bibliographical references and index.
  Summary: "Middle school readers will find out about the important world, national, and cultural developments of the decade 1950-1959"—Provided by publisher.
  ISBN-13: 978-0-7660-3134-0
  ISBN-10: 0-7660-3134-9
  1. United States—History—1945-1953—Pictorial works—Juvenile literature. 2. United States—History—1953-1961—Pictorial works—Juvenile literature. 3. History, Modern—20th century—Pictorial works—Juvenile literature. 4. Nineteen fifties—Pictorial works—Juvenile literature.
I. Title. II. Title: Nineteen fifties decade in photos.
  E813.C67 2009
  973.921—dc22

                                                                            2008042994

Printed in the United States of America.

092009 Lake Book Manufacturing, Inc., Melrose Park, IL

10 9 8 7 6 5 4 3 2 1

To Our Readers: We have done our best to make sure all Internet Addresses in this book were active and appropriate when we went to press. However, the author and the publisher have no control over and assume no liability for the material available on those Internet sites or on other Web sites they may link to. Any comments or suggestions can be sent by email to comments@enslow.com or to the address on the back cover.

Every effort has been made to locate all copyright holders of material used in this book. If any errors or omissions have occurred, corrections will be made in future editions of this book.

♻ Enslow Publishers, Inc., is committed to printing our books on recycled paper. The paper in every book contains 10% to 30% post-consumer waste (PCW). The cover board on the outside of each book contains 100% PCW. Our goal is to do our part to help young people and the environment too!

Produced by OTTN Publishing, Stockton, N.J.

TABLE OF CONTENTS

The decade 1950–1959 is often considered a happy and pleasant time in which fathers worked while mothers stayed home and raised their children. However, this idealized image ignores the many real problems Americans faced during the 1950s.

WELCOME TO THE 1950s

During the 1950s, Americans experienced a wave of prosperity. The previous two decades had been marked by a world war and economic disaster. The 1950s were different. Many Americans were able to build careers and raise their families comfortably. New technology made life easier. New medical advances saved lives. Television was also new. It offered hours of entertainment. Americans enjoyed their newfound affluence.

World War II had changed the world forever. That enormous conflict ended in 1945. In the years that followed, Europe and Asia struggled to rebuild.

Two men program the enormous UNIVAC computer, mid-1950s. UNIVAC, which stood for "**U**niversal **A**utomatic **C**omputer," was the first electronic computer available for sale to businesses and schools. The computer was so large that it took up an entire room and weighed more than thirteen tons.

When the Soviet Union developed atomic weapons, Americans worried about the possibility of nuclear war. In many communities, fallout shelters were constructed in the basements of public buildings during the 1950s. These were places where people could go to protect themselves in case of a nuclear attack. Fallout shelters were indicated by signs like the one on the left in this photo.

America emerged from the war stronger than ever. The United States helped its allies—and even its former enemies—to recover. America also grew into a superpower. A superpower is a very strong country that leads other nations.

America was not the only superpower in the 1950s. The Soviet Union was also very strong. The United States and the Soviet Union had been allies during World War II. Their alliance did not last long. The two nations held different beliefs. The Soviet Union was based on an idea called communism, which Soviet leaders wanted to spread around the world.

Under communism, no single person owned property. Instead, everyone shared it. All people were supposed to work together for the common good. To make communism function, the Soviet government forced its citizens to follow many rules.

This system clashed sharply with the American ideals of liberty and independence. The Soviet goal of spreading communism around the world worried many Americans. They feared that communist spies were living among them.

A bitter rivalry grew between the United States and the Soviet Union. Each tried to gain an advantage over the other. Each sought out other countries to serve as allies. The superpowers also built huge armies in case of war. Yet both sides knew that a war between them would be extremely dangerous. America and the Soviet Union both had nuclear bombs. A single nuclear bomb could destroy most of a city. If used, those terrifying weapons might wipe out all of humanity.

The two superpowers carefully avoided a direct conflict. Instead, they found other ways to fight. Their struggle came to be known as the Cold War.

African-American and white schoolchildren get into line together at a Washington, D.C., school, 1955. In May 1954, the U.S. Supreme Court ruled in *Brown v. Board of Education of Topeka, Kansas* that it was unconstitutional to force African Americans to attend separate public schools from white students. The court later ruled that public schools should be desegregated "with all deliberate speed."

American and Soviet diplomats argued in the United Nations, or UN. The UN was created after World War II. Its purpose was to help countries resolve their differences peacefully—though often this goal was not achieved. In 1950, the UN faced its first Cold War crisis. The Soviet Union's ally North Korea invaded the U.S. ally South Korea. United Nations troops from around the world went to Korea to stop them. The bloody Korean War would drag on for three years.

While American and other soldiers fought in Korea, changes were taking place in the United States. African Americans were demanding equal rights. Teens danced to a new music called rock and roll. Men and women were getting married and having children at a high rate. The surge in births was called the "baby boom." These events would reshape American society. Trends that began in the 1950s are still affecting the nation today.

Marilyn Monroe (1926–1962) was one of the most popular entertainers of the 1950s. She starred in such films as *Gentlemen Prefer Blondes* (1953) and *The Seven Year Itch* (1955). Her 1959 film *Some Like it Hot* is considered one of the greatest comedies of all time.

These figures representing American soldiers are part of a memorial to veterans of the Korean War. More than 1.7 million American servicemen were involved in the 1951–1953 conflict.

FIGHTING ERUPTS IN KOREA

Korea is located in east Asia. It is a peninsula, which means it juts out into the water. (The state of Florida is another example of a peninsula.) In 1950, Korea became a battleground. It was home to the first major conflict of the Cold War.

Korea's troubles began just as World War II was ending. During the war, Japan occupied this land. However, Japan was defeated in 1945. At that time, American troops took control of the southern half of Korea. Soviet troops took control of the northern half. Korea was divided. South Korea became an ally of the United States. North Korea became a communist state and was supported by the Soviet Union.

As America and the Soviet Union grew more hostile toward each other, so did North and South Korea. In June 1950, North Korea's army suddenly invaded South Korea. The surprise attack shocked the world.

Two days after North Korea's invasion began, President Harry S. Truman committed U.S. troops to defend South Korea. In a June 27, 1950, statement announcing the policy, Truman said, "The attack upon Korea makes it plain beyond all doubt that Communism has passed beyond the use of subversion to conquer independent nations and will now use armed invasion and war."

The United Nations demanded an end to the invasion. North Korea refused. Instead, it sent more tanks and troops into South Korea.

U.S. president Harry Truman faced a difficult decision. He desperately wanted to help defend South Korea from the brutal attack. He knew that, if conquered, South Korea would surely become communist. Truman wished to stop the spread of communism around the world. To do so, he would need to send U.S. troops to Korea. Yet America was not ready to fight another war.

U.S. troops are pictured on a pier after debarking from their ship in Korea, August 1950. The American soldiers were sent to Korea as part of a United Nations force.

An African-American sergeant points out a North Korean position to his squad, 1950. In Korea, unlike in previous American wars, soldiers of all racial backgrounds fought together in integrated units. Two years earlier, President Truman had signed executive order 9981, which desegregated the military.

World War II had ended just five years earlier. Americans were enjoying the peace. They focused on raising families, going to school, and working at jobs.

President Truman decided to commit U.S. forces to help South Korea. Many other nations agreed that this was the right thing to do. They also sent troops to Korea. In all, twenty-two countries from the United Nations volunteered to assist South Korea. Led by America, the UN forces hoped to halt the invasion. But North Korea had allies too. The Soviet Union provided North Korea's soldiers with weapons and training. Communist China would also come to the aid of the North.

The first few months of the war went badly for the UN troops. They could not stop the North Korean attack. They were pushed back to a tiny corner at the tip of the peninsula. The outlook was grim. If they could not hang on, the UN soldiers would lose the war.

McCarthy Fuels the Red Scare

In the 1950s, many people feared communism. The Soviet Union threatened to spread the communist revolution around the world. Communist soldiers were on the attack in Korea. A handful of American citizens were arrested for giving atomic secrets to the Soviets. People worried that other communist spies were living in the United States. This widespread panic came to be known as the Red Scare.

Joseph McCarthy was a U.S. senator from Wisconsin. He used the nation's fear of communism to gain power for himself. McCarthy became famous by accusing others. He held public hearings to question people he suspected of being communists. Generally, he had little or no proof. The McCarthy hearings

During the late 1940s and early 1950s, Americans were alarmed by the Soviet Union's oppression of eastern Europe and by the rise to power of an unfriendly communist government in China. Books like *Is This Tomorrow?* (1947) and movies like *Invasion USA* (1952) fueled concerns that communists were secretly working hard to destroy American society.

IS THIS TOMORROW

AMERICA UNDER COMMUNISM!

WB055 DL PD

RENO NEV FEB 11 1139A

The White House
Washington

THE PRESIDENT

THE WHITE HOUSE   1950 FEB 11 PM 7 31

IN A LINCOLN DAY SPEECH AT WHEELING THURSDAY NIGHT

I STATED THAT THE STATE DEPARTMENT HARBORS A NEST OF

COMMUNISTS AND COMMUNIST SYMPATHIZERS WHO ARE HELPING TO

SHAPE OUR FOREIGN POLICY. I FURTHER STATED THAT I HAVE IN

MY POSSESSION THE NAMES OF 57 COMMUNISTS WHO ARE IN THE

STATE DEPARTMENT AT PRESENT. A STATE DEPARTMENT SPOKESMAN

Telegram from McCarthy to President Truman, claiming to know of fifty-seven Communists working for the U.S. government. Although McCarthy never provided any proof, his claim attracted national attention at a time when American fear of the Soviet Union was growing.

ruined many lives. The people he questioned became outcasts. Some lost their jobs because of Joseph McCarthy's unproven claims. In Hollywood, actors, directors, and screenwriters suspected of being communists were prevented from working.

By 1954, a few people began to take on McCarthy publicly. Journalist Edward R. Murrow hosted a TV show that exposed the Wisconsin senator's dirty tactics. Senator Ralph Flanders of Vermont spoke out against McCarthy in the U.S. Senate. McCarthy's power waned. The Senate punished him for his reckless charges. He slowly disappeared from public life and died in 1957. The fear and mistrust of the Red Scare gradually declined.

Senator Joseph McCarthy (1908-1957) is pictured in 1954, during his investigation of communists in the U.S. Army. The hearings were broadcast on television and radio, allowing Americans to see and hear Joseph McCarthy in action for the first time. Many observers did not like his bullying tactics and failure to provide proof of his allegations.

Tuning in to Television

*T*elevision became a part of American life in the 1950s. Before then, radio was the most popular form of entertainment. The major radio networks were NBC, CBS, and ABC. In the late 1940s, these networks made the move to television. Sales of TV sets soared.

A family watches a program about pioneers on television, circa 1950. During the 1950s, television shows and movies about the West were very popular. These included *The Roy Rogers Show*, *The Lone Ranger*, and *Gunsmoke*.

The police drama *Dragnet* was one of the most popular shows of the 1950s. The program's star, Jack Webb (right), had originally created *Dragnet* for radio in the late 1940s. The television show ran from 1951 until 1959, then was revived in the late 1960s.

Early television was much different from the TV we know today. There were very few channels. Color TV was not yet available, so all shows were in black-and-white. There was no way to record or save programs in the home. Still, people prized television. For the first time, they could watch moving images from the comfort of home.

Some of the most popular radio programs went on to become TV shows. One was the famous soap opera *Guiding Light*, which still airs today. Other shows were made just for television. In 1950, CBS debuted a game show called *What's My Line?* It ran for decades. A year later came the comedy *I Love Lucy*. Starring Lucille Ball, it remains one of the most beloved shows in TV history.

Comedienne Lucille Ball (1911–1989) receives a kiss on the cheek from her husband, Cuban-born bandleader and musician Desi Arnaz (1917–1986), on the set of their television series, *I Love Lucy*. The show won many awards, and influenced other television comedies.

U.S. Forces Land at Inchon

Before 1950, many Americans had never heard of Korea. Suddenly, U.S. troops were fighting a war in that distant land. Even worse, the American soldiers and their allies were losing. North Korean forces controlled nearly the entire peninsula. A famous American general named Douglas MacArthur was

American marines use scaling ladders to climb ashore during the amphibious invasion at Inchon, September 15, 1950. The attack was so swift that casualties were surprisingly low.

General Courtney Whitney, General Douglas MacArthur, and General Edward M. Almond observe the shelling of Inchon from the *U.S.S. Mount McKinley.*

in charge of the UN troops. MacArthur did not panic. In fact, he had a plan for victory.

The North Korean army had chased the UN troops all the way to the tip of the peninsula. The North Koreans were far away from home. They were running low on food and ammunition. MacArthur wanted to surprise them by attacking from behind. In September 1950, he put seventy thousand American soldiers aboard a fleet of ships. Their mission was to sail up the coast of the peninsula. They would then come ashore behind the North Korean army and launch an attack.

The U.S. troops landed at the harbor city of Inchon. They rushed inland and quickly caught the enemy soldiers by surprise. The North Koreans retreated for the safety of home. MacArthur's plan had worked. However, the war was far from finished. Many more battles lay ahead.

U.S. soldiers are on patrol between destroyed buildings during the Inchon invasion.

HERE COME THE BABY BOOMERS

The 1950s were a time of prosperity. Previous decades had been much more difficult. The Great Depression lasted through the 1930s. World War II raged during the first half of the 1940s. When that war finally ended, people were eager to build happy, peaceful lives. They married and started families. In 1946, America's population began to grow rapidly. More than 3.4 million

Portrait of a young couple with their child, 1950s.

A Chinese-American family eats traditional foods in a San Francisco restaurant, 1956. During the Baby Boom years, all ethnic groups in the United States saw an increase in birth rate.

babies were born in the United States that year, up from 2.8 million in 1945. By 1954, more than 4 million babies were being born each year. The nation was experiencing a baby boom.

The baby boom lasted until 1964. During the nineteen years of the baby boom, over 76 million babies were born. Society scrambled to keep up with their needs. For example, new schools had to be built quickly for the growing number of students.

When the boomers grew up, they too began having children. This created a second, smaller baby boom. Currently, the first boomers are reaching retirement age. As they leave the workforce, there will be many jobs to fill. Throughout their lives, the baby boomers have shaped American culture because of their large numbers.

Members of an African-American family photographed in their dining room. According to the U.S. Census Bureau, the African-American population rose from about 15 million in 1950 to over 18.8 million in 1960.

A wounded chaplain performs a memorial service over the snow-covered bodies of dead American marines. This photo was taken near Koto-ri, Korea, on December 3, 1950, as the UN force was reeling from the Chinese army's surprise attack.

CHINA ENTERS THE KOREAN WAR

Events in Korea were unfolding rapidly. At the start of the war, the invading North Korean soldiers seemed unstoppable. They raced deep into South Korea and nearly won total victory. Then came General Douglas MacArthur's surprise attack at Inchon. It shocked the North Korean troops. They retreated home in panic.

American soldiers and a tank take a defensive position, 1950.

South Korea was free of invaders. Yet General MacArthur was not satisfied. MacArthur wanted to invade North Korea and destroy its army. Only then, he believed, would South Korea be safe. United Nations troops crossed into North Korea in October 1950. They advanced quickly. MacArthur stated confidently that the war would be over by Christmas 1950.

North Korea and China are neighbors. China had just become a communist state in 1949. Its leaders worried about the approaching UN forces. They feared that the UN troops might not stop with North Korea. An attack on China might be next, they feared. The Chinese government issued stern warnings not to

United Nations forces withdraw from Pyongyang, the North Korean capital, after China's entry into the war in late 1950. The UN troops were pushed back across the 38th parallel, the border between North and South Korea.

The 1950s Decade in Photos: "The American Decade"

Three American F-86 Sabres fly on patrol over North Korea. American pilots distinguished themselves in aerial combat with Soviet-built MiG-15 jet fighters during the war. Many of the dogfights took place near the Yalu River, an area that became known as MiG Alley.

approach its border. Meanwhile, the UN soldiers kept getting closer. China prepared for war.

In late November 1950, some UN troops approached the Yalu River. The river served as the border between North Korea and China. It appeared that the war was over. North Korea was beaten. Just then, China's huge army attacked. The Chinese soldiers greatly outnumbered the UN soldiers. General MacArthur's troops retreated in chaos. The Chinese assault pushed them back into South Korea. A shocked MacArthur said that it was an entirely new war.

GENERAL DOUGLAS MACARTHUR

Douglas MacArthur was born in 1880. His father had been a Civil War hero. From the time he was a boy, Douglas wanted to be an army officer too. He attended the U.S. Military Academy at West Point, New York. Later, he led troops into battle during World War I. During World War II, MacArthur helped defeat Japan in the Pacific.

When the Korean War broke out, MacArthur was already seventy years old. Clearly, Korea would be the last war of his career. MacArthur desperately wanted to win it.

THE ROSENBERGS ARE EXECUTED

*I*n the 1940s, American scientists built the world's first atomic bomb. It was a very powerful weapon. A single atomic bomb could destroy much of a city. The atomic bomb helped end World War II. Japan surrendered after U.S. planes struck two of its cities with atomic bombs.

America was anxious to keep its bomb design a secret. However, in 1949, the Soviet Union built its own atomic bomb. Suddenly, America's Cold War enemy became an even greater threat to the United States.

Investigators soon learned that spies had given America's atomic bomb secrets to the Soviets. A handful of people were arrested. They included Julius and Ethel Rosenberg. The Rosenbergs were a married couple from New York. They believed in communism.

During World War II, Julius Rosenberg had begun spying for the Soviet Union, which was then America's ally. Ethel Rosenberg's brother, David Greenglass, was in the army. In 1944, Greenglass was sent to Los Alamos, New Mexico. There, he worked as a machinist in the top-secret facility where the atomic bomb was being developed. Julius Rosenberg soon convinced his brother-in-law to pass along information about the atomic bomb program.

In 1951, when the Rosenbergs went on trial, David Greenglass was one of the main witnesses for the prosecution. Greenglass told

This photo shows a nuclear weapon being tested in the mid-1950s.

Ethel Rosenberg's brother, David Greenglass (left), is handcuffed and accompanied by a U.S. Marshal in this June 1950 photo. During World War II, Greenglass had worked on the Manhattan Project, the secret U.S. operation that created the first atomic bombs. After his arrest, Greenglass admitted that he had given his brother-in-law, Julius Rosenberg, atomic secrets for the Soviets.

how he had given top-secret information to Julius Rosenberg. He said Ethel had once typed up his handwritten notes to pass along to the Soviets. That was the only evidence against her. The Rosenbergs insisted they were innocent, but they were both found guilty and sentenced to die in the electric chair.

The Rosenberg case divided America. Many people believed the two were innocent. Also, the couple had two young sons, and many Americans did not want to see the boys orphaned by the execution of their parents. After their legal appeals failed, however, the Rosenbergs were put to death on June 19, 1953.

Today, the case remains controversial. It is known that Julius Rosenberg did, in fact, spy for the Soviet Union. But whether Ethel was involved remains in doubt. David Greenglass has since said that he lied about his sister's role.

Greenglass claims he did so in exchange for the government's agreement not to charge his wife, Ruth. Ruth Greenglass had been an occasional messenger in the spy ring. Debate also continues about the punishment given to the Rosenbergs. A half dozen people were convicted of passing atomic secrets to the Soviets, but only the Rosenbergs were executed.

Ethel and Julius Rosenberg are separated by a wire screen as they are transported to Sing Sing Prison. In March 1951, the Rosenbergs were found guilty of conspiracy to commit espionage. They were executed for the crime on June 19, 1953.

The Rosenbergs Are Executed

TRUMAN FIRES MacARTHUR

General Douglas MacArthur had nearly defeated North Korea. It was to be the final victory of his brilliant career. Then China suddenly entered the Korean War. The Chinese onslaught ruined MacArthur's plans for a quick victory. He prepared for a long fight with China.

President Harry S. Truman watched the events in Korea carefully. Like MacArthur, he wanted to win the war. However, Truman also wanted to make sure that the fighting stayed inside Korea. He could not allow the conflict to grow into World War III. America and China's ally, the Soviet Union, both had atomic weapons. Truman knew that another world war could destroy humankind. For this reason, Truman ordered MacArthur to limit the fighting to Korea.

General Douglas MacArthur meets with President Harry S. Truman on Wake Island, October 1950. Six months later, Truman would remove MacArthur from command of the UN forces in South Korea.

MacArthur did not agree with the idea of a limited war. He believed that America should do everything possible to win. MacArthur argued that the war should be expanded into China. He even spoke about the possibility of dropping atomic bombs on that country. For months, Truman and MacArthur argued over the best way to fight the war in Korea. In the United States, final authority for military decisions rests with the president. Truman believed that, by resisting his orders, MacArthur was undermining civilian control of the military. At last, in April 1951, the president fired MacArthur. Another general, Matthew Ridgway, took over in Korea.

Despite his defiance of President Truman, Douglas MacArthur remained very popular in the United States. He returned home to a hero's welcome.

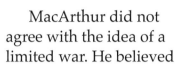

MacArthur received a ticker-tape parade in New York City on April 20, 1951. At the time, Truman's action removing MacArthur was very unpopular. Today, however, most historians agree that Truman made the right decision.

National flags fly outside the New York headquarters of the United Nations. One of the UN's goals was to oversee decolonization— the peaceful breakup of colonial empires. The UN Trusteeship Council was created to ease the transition of colonies in Africa, Asia, and elsewhere into independent countries.

GAINING INDEPENDENCE

A colony is a territory ruled by a distant nation. (The United States began as thirteen British colonies but won independence as a result of the Revolutionary War.)

At the end of World War II, there were still many colonies around the world. Parts of Asia and almost all of Africa were controlled by European countries,

On this 1950s-era map of the world, independent states are colored red (if they were members of the United Nations) or white (for non-members). Colonies—territories ruled by a European country like Great Britain or France—are labeled in green. Countries that by 1950 were part of the UN's trusteeship system, and therefore being prepared for self-rule, are marked in blue. The green bands around India/Pakistan and the Philippines indicate that these countries have already gained their independence.

mainly Britain and France. But people in the colonies wished to be free from foreign rule. And during the 1950s, the drive for self-rule gathered steam.

During World War II, Britain and France had fought together on the side of the Allies. The Allies were fighting to defend freedom. So it was only natural that people in the British and French colonies would also demand

A member of the French Foreign Legion walks along a rice paddy during a patrol through communist-held areas in Vietnam, 1954. That year, the decisive battle at Dien Bien Phu forced France to give up its colony in Vietnam.

Officials of Britain's African colony known as Gold Coast meet with Dr. Ralph Bunche (left), director of the UN Trusteeship Council, and UN secretary-general Trygvie Lie (center) in 1951. When Gold Coast gained independence as Ghana in 1957, Kwame Nkrumah (second from left) would become the country's first president.

their freedom. But leaders in Britain and France did not grant independence to their colonies right away, or without a struggle. In India, however, an independence movement led by Mohandas Gandhi finally helped convince Britain to let go of its largest and most important colony in 1947. Other British colonies in Asia quickly followed.

France tried to restore its control over southeast Asia after World War II but faced violent resistance. Cambodia won independence in 1953. Vietnamese fighters defeated the French the following year.

In Africa, people in the colonies labored for freedom in a variety of ways. In some places there were strikes and protests. In other places there were armed uprisings. By the end of the 1950s, a handful of African nations—including Morocco, Tunisia, and Ghana—had gained independence. Most of the continent would follow during the next decade.

KOREAN WAR ENDS IN A DRAW

By the fall of 1952, the Korean War was already two years old. Tens of thousands of American soldiers had been killed or wounded in the war. Yet there seemed to be little progress on the battlefield. The United Nations troops and their communist foes had fought to a draw. Brutal fighting continued along the 38th parallel, the dividing line between North and South Korea. But neither side could score a major victory. A retired U.S. general believed it was time to end the war.

Dwight D. Eisenhower was one of America's finest military leaders. During World War II, he helped defeat Nazi Germany. Afterward, he retired

President Dwight D. Eisenhower (second from left) reviews troops in South Korea, fulfilling a campaign promise.

Reporters interview General William K. Harrison, the UN's representative, after a cease-fire meeting at Panmunjom, Korea, in May 1953. An armistice, or agreement to stop fighting, was signed on July 27 of that year.

from the army. In 1952, Eisenhower decided to run for president. He told voters that, if elected, he would go to Korea. He wanted to find a way to stop the fighting. Americans were tired of the costly war. They elected Eisenhower to the presidency.

Eisenhower kept his promise and traveled to Korea. He quickly saw that neither side could win. As president, he made it clear to North Korea and China that the United Nations wanted peace. He forcefully added that South Korea must never be attacked again. After months of talks, both sides agreed to a truce. The fighting in Korea finally came to an end in July 1953. The war had claimed the lives of more than 2.5 million soldiers, including more than thirty-five thousand Americans.

An American sergeant watches a South Korean soldier break down an M-16 rifle. Since the Korean conflict ended, the United States has maintained a military presence in South Korea. Today, nearly thirty thousand U.S. servicemen remain stationed in that country.

RISE OF THE BEAT GENERATION

America prospered during the 1950s. Yet not everyone was happy with American society. Some people believed that Americans were too concerned about owning a lot of things, and too concerned with what other people thought of them. A group of writers known as the Beats rejected the values of mainstream society. They wrote about topics that shocked typical readers, such as drug use.

The most famous Beat writer was Jack Kerouac. He wrote a novel called *On the Road*. It was based on his wild adventures as a hitchhiker. *On the Road* was published in 1957. At the time, it offended many people. Today, the book is considered an important work of American literature.

The Beat writers inspired many other people who were dissatisfied with American society. Some of

Jack Kerouac (1922–1969) became a best-selling author when his book *On the Road* was published in 1957. The book included references to many of Kerouac's friends, who became known as the Beats.

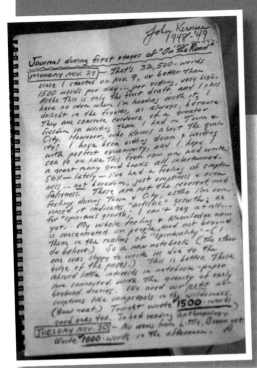

This page is from a journal kept by Jack Kerouac from 1948 to 1949. It was written at the time he was starting to compose the text that would become *On The Road*.

these people came to be called beatniks. They liked to look different from everyone else. Many men grew a beard known as a goatee. They also wore a hat called a beret. Beatnik women liked to dress in black. They wore their hair long and straight. Whereas most Americans were fascinated by television, beatniks thought TV was ruining the nation. Like the Beat Generation writers, they preferred jazz music and poetry.

Allen Ginsberg (1926-1997) reads his most famous poem, "Howl," outside of a U.S. government building in Washington, D.C. "Howl" attempted to capture the experiences and attitudes of the Beat movement in verse. It was very controversial when it was published in 1956.

Rise of the Beat Generation

MEDICAL MARVELS

The 1950s saw remarkable advances in medicine. For the first time, doctors were able to treat many deadly diseases. One of those diseases was polio. Polio is caused by a virus. It can cripple or kill its victims, who are often children. In 1952, Jonas Salk created a vaccine for polio. Vaccines help the body resist disease. After extensive testing, Salk's vaccine was found to be safe and effective. It began to be administered widely in 1955. The vaccine quickly stopped the spread of polio in America and elsewhere.

Before the 1950s, operating on the heart was nearly impossible. The heart pumps blood through the body. If the heart stopped beating during surgery, the patient would die. In 1953, an American doctor named John Gibbon solved that problem. He invented a heart-lung machine.

A young child crippled by polio—both his legs are in braces—asks for donations to a new polio hospital, circa 1950. Polio epidemics were common during the first half of the twentieth century. The epidemics left thousands of children and adults paralyzed.

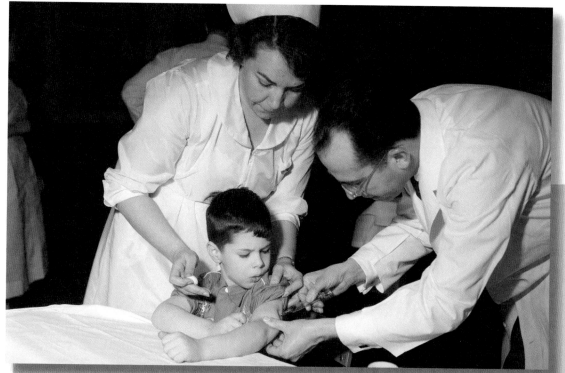

A nurse holds a young patient while Dr. Jonas Salk (1914–1995) administers the polio vaccine. Salk's vaccine helped to greatly reduce cases of polio in the United States.

The device pumped blood through the patient's body. It allowed doctors to stop the heart so they could operate on it. Today, open-heart surgery is common.

The first successful organ transplant took place in 1954. Dr. Joseph Murray of Boston, Massachusetts, performed the surgery. His patient needed a new kidney. Murray transplanted a kidney donated by the patient's twin brother.

Dr. John H. Gibbon Jr. (1903–1973) performed the first successful open-heart surgery at Philadelphia's Thomas Jefferson University in 1953.

ROSA PARKS FIGHTS SEGREGATION

Segregation is the practice of keeping people separate. In the 1950s, some southern states still had laws to segregate black people and white people. A black woman named Rosa Parks fought to change those laws.

Rosa Parks lived in Montgomery, Alabama. She often rode the bus to work. In Montgomery, black passengers were forced to ride in the back of the bus. On December 1, 1955, Parks was sitting in the first row of seats designated for black riders. The whites-only section in front of her filled up, so the bus driver told her to move. He wanted to give her seat to a white man. Rosa Parks refused. She felt that she was being treated unfairly.

The police arrested Parks for breaking the law. She was jailed and fined $10. The incident

A policeman in Montgomery, Alabama, fingerprints Rosa Parks (1913–2005). She was arrested in 1955 for violating segregation laws.

Members of the African-American community in Montgomery listen as Reverend Martin Luther King, Jr., discusses the bus boycott, 1956. Rosa Parks is seated in the center of the front row.

outraged Montgomery's other black citizens. To protest, they stopped riding the city buses. A young minister named Dr. Martin Luther King, Jr., was their leader. He would become a national figure in the growing struggle for racial equality. In later years, Rosa Parks received many honors for her courage. She died in 2005 at age ninety-two.

Rosa Parks prepares to board a bus at the end of the Montgomery bus boycott, December 26, 1956.

HITTING THE HIGHWAYS

The booming U.S. economy meant that there were more cars on the road than ever. However, many of the nation's roads were in poor condition and were too narrow for easy travel. In 1956, President Dwight D. Eisenhower proposed a huge highway system. (Highways are long, straight roads meant for high-speed driving.) The project changed the way Americans lived and traveled.

The American system of interstate highways was inspired by President Eisenhower's experiences as a soldier. Eisenhower believed that the United States needed good roads for national defense. A highway system would allow troops and supplies to be moved quickly wherever they were needed.

President Eisenhower (center, wearing hat) participates in a ribbon-cutting ceremony opening a new section of interstate highway, November 1959.

Today, America's interstate highways are part of the world's largest and most complex road system. Interstate highways connect nearly all major cities in the continental United States.

Eisenhower knew America needed better roads. As a young army officer, he once drove across the country. The trip was slow and difficult. Later, as a general in Europe, he was amazed by Germany's efficient highways. The large roads made transportation much easier.

In 1956, President Eisenhower signed the Federal-Aid Highway Act. In the thirty-five years that followed, America built the world's largest highway network. It is roughly forty-five thousand miles long and crisscrosses the entire nation. America's interstate highway system is named in Eisenhower's honor.

United Nations troops arrive in Port Said, Egypt, to restore order during the 1956 Suez Canel crisis.

THE SUEZ CRISIS

A canal is a man-made waterway connecting two larger bodies of water. It serves as a shortcut for ships. They sail through the canal to avoid long trips around land.

The Suez Canal is in Egypt. It connects the Mediterranean Sea with the Red Sea. The Suez Canal gives ships easy access between Europe and Asia.

Egyptian president Gamal Abdel Nasser (1918–1970) claimed that the Suez Canal was Egypt's property.

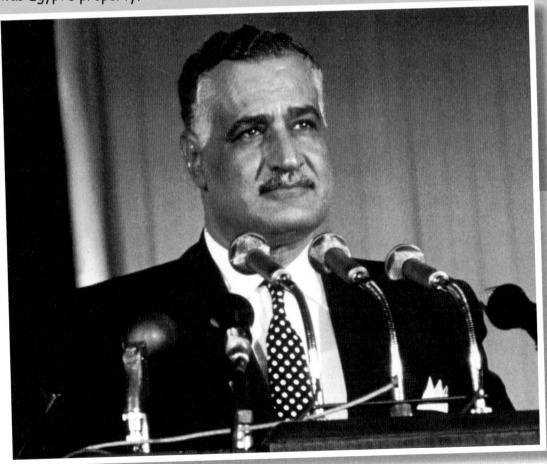

Israeli soldiers attend a briefing before going into action, October 1956. The Israeli army attacked Egyptian troops in the Sinai Peninsula, while British and French paratroopers captured the canal.

Without it, ships would need to sail all the way around Africa. In 1956, a major crisis developed over this key waterway.

The Suez Canal was built in the mid-1800s. Egypt was controlled by the British, so Britain also controlled the canal. The British allowed ships of all nations to use it. In 1956, an independent Egypt seized the canal. The takeover alarmed Britain, France, and Israel. They feared that Egypt would close the waterway to nations it did not like. Already, Israeli ships were banned from using the Suez Canal.

Egypt's president was Gamal Abdel Nasser. He refused to give up control of the Suez Canal. He said it was Egyptian property. On October 29, 1956, Israel launched a surprise attack against Egypt. It was part of a secret plan between Israel, Britain, and France to capture the canal and punish Nasser. A week after the Israeli invasion, British and French forces attacked Egypt as well. The Egyptian army was unable to stop them. Nasser chose to deprive the invaders of their prize. He purposely sank forty ships inside the canal. The sunken hulls blocked any ships from using the waterway.

The rest of the world watched the Suez crisis with alarm. As with Korea, there was concern that it could grow into a world war. The United Nations decided to act. The world body ordered a halt to the fighting. It then sent its own troops—known as peacekeepers—to the canal. They restored order. Within two months, control of the Suez Canal was returned to Egypt. UN workers removed the sunken ships. The canal reopened to shipping in early 1957.

Dutch salvage vessels raise one of the ships that Nasser had ordered to be sunk to block the Suez Canal, 1957.

ROCK AND ROLL ARRIVES

Little Richard was one of the most popular rock-and-roll stars of the 1950s. His hits included "Tutti Frutti," "Lucille," "Long Tall Sally," and "Keep a-Knockin' (but You Can't Come In)."

A new style of music became popular in the 1950s. It was called rock and roll. The new music had a lively beat and catchy lyrics. Rock and roll grew from African-American music, especially rhythm and blues. A new instrument known as the electric guitar also helped give rock and roll its start.

The first rock-and-roll hit was "Rock Around the Clock" in 1955. Bill Haley and the Comets performed it. Teens enjoyed the song's snappy melody. Before long, there were many famous rock-and-roll artists. Chuck Berry scored hits with "Roll Over Beethoven" in 1956 and "Johnny B. Goode" in 1958. Buddy Holly sang "Peggy Sue" in 1957. Little Richard's "Good Golly Miss Molly," another rock-and-roll classic, was released in 1958.

Elvis Presley was the biggest rock-and-roll star to emerge in the 1950s. He was

Rock-and-roll music had a huge impact on American fashion, attitudes, and social behaviors during the 1950s. Many adults believed the new music encouraged rebellious conduct among teenagers.

born in Mississippi in 1935. Presley taught himself to play the guitar. At age twenty-two, he already had five number-one songs. They included "Hound Dog" and "Don't Be Cruel." Elvis would go on to notch thirty number-one hits in his career. He also starred in movies. Elvis Presley became one of the most famous entertainers in the world. Rock-and-roll fans still remember him fondly as "the King."

Rock-and-roll legends Bill Haley (1925–1981) and Elvis Presley (1935–1977) pose together after a 1955 performance. Haley's 1954 song "Rock Around the Clock" was one of the genre's first big hits. Presley became the most popular musician of the 1950s, recording hits like "Don't Be Cruel" and "Jailhouse Rock."

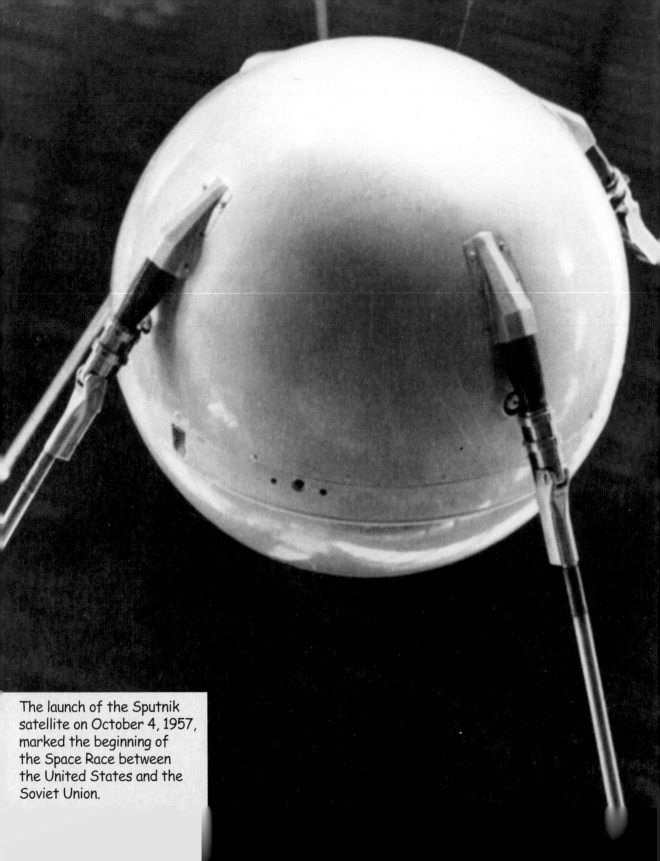

The launch of the Sputnik
satellite on October 4, 1957,
marked the beginning of
the Space Race between
the United States and the
Soviet Union.

SPUTNIK LAUNCHES THE SPACE RACE

Today, humans visit space regularly. Astronauts have walked on the moon. A crew lives in orbit aboard the International Space Station. Robot spacecraft have been sent to other planets in our solar system. All of these feats are relatively recent. Before 1957, humanity had never ventured into space.

In that year, the Soviet Union launched the first man-made object into orbit. It was a satellite called *Sputnik 1*. The amazing feat fascinated the world. It also started a heated competition between the Soviet Union and the United States. People called this competition the Space Race. It was a positive outcome of the Cold War.

Sputnik 1 weighed less than two hundred pounds. A Soviet rocket carried it into space on

Launch of the first American satellite, *Explorer 1*, in 1958.

The Vanguard satellite, launched in March 1958, was the second U.S. satellite in orbit. Although *Vanguard I* is no longer functioning, it is expected to remain in earth orbit for two more centuries.

October 4, 1957. One month later, the Soviets launched the larger *Sputnik 2* satellite. A dog named Laika was placed aboard the craft. (*Laika* means "barker" in Russian.) She became the world's first space traveler. Sadly, Laika did not survive her trip. The heat and stress of the event killed her. Regardless, the two Sputnik launches impressed people. The Soviet Union had taken an early lead in the Space Race.

The U.S. government was alarmed. Soviet rockets were powerful enough to carry objects into space. It seemed likely that those same rockets could be used to attack the United States. President Eisenhower decided to boost

America's space program. He created the National Aeronautics and Space Administration, or NASA. The new agency would manage the nation's spaceflight efforts.

America put its own satellite in space on January 31, 1958. Known as *Explorer 1*, it would stay in orbit for twelve years. Regardless, the Soviets stayed ahead in the Space Race. They learned how to keep dogs alive during trips into space. Soon they would attempt to send a human into orbit.

In 1959, the newly created National Aeronautics and Space Administration (NASA) introduced Project Mercury. This was NASA's first human spaceflight program. Seven experienced test pilots were chosen as Project Mercury's astronauts. They included (left to right) Scott Carpenter, L. Gordon Cooper, John H. Glenn Jr., Virgil I. "Gus" Grissom, Walter H. "Wally" Schirra, Alan B. Shepard Jr., and Donald K. "Deke" Slayton.

CASTRO SEIZES POWER IN CUBA

Cuba is an island nation. It is located less than a hundred miles south of Florida. Cuba and the United States share a long history together. For many years, the two nations were very friendly toward each other. However, that friendship ended abruptly in the 1950s.

In 1952, an army officer named Fulgencio Batista seized control of the Cuban government. Batista was a brutal and corrupt dictator. He was very unpopular. Batista stayed in power only by using violence against the Cuban people.

Several groups wanted to overthrow Batista. One was led by a young lawyer named Fidel Castro. In 1956, Castro gathered his small band of rebels in the rugged mountains of eastern Cuba. Castro promised to help Cuba's poor people. He also said he would restore freedom. Gradually, Castro attracted more followers. In 1958, Batista sent his army into the mountains to destroy Castro's rebels. But it was the Cuban

Cuban rebel leader Fidel Castro, seated and holding a rifle, is backed up by two armed followers at their hideout in eastern Cuba. During the 1950s, Castro led a rebellion against Cuba's government.

Today, the image of Ernesto "Che" Guevara appears on the Ministry of the Interior building in Havana, Cuba. Guevara (1928–1967) played an important part in the rebel conquest of Cuba.

army that got beaten. On January 1, 1959, Batista fled the country. Castro then took power. His revolution had succeeded.

Castro declared that America held too much control over Cuba. His government seized land owned by U.S. companies. Castro turned Cuba into a communist nation. He became an ally of the Soviet Union.

Cubans who disliked communism fled to Florida. America stopped all trade with Castro's government. In coming years, a defiant Cuba would continue to make headlines. One crisis would push the world to the brink of nuclear war.

Fidel Castro addresses a session of the United Nations. After seizing control of Cuba in 1959, Castro served as the country's ruler until 2008.

GOLDEN AGE OF SCIENCE FICTION

*T*ales about the future are called science fiction. They describe adventures that are currently impossible. Stories about aliens, time travel, and space battles are examples of science fiction. In the 1950s, many great science fiction authors were writing their best stories.

Science fiction movies such as *The Blob* (1958) became very popular during the 1950s.

Some people believe the 1956 film *Invasion of the Body Snatchers* is a satire about the emotional barrenness of suburban life.

Isaac Asimov was born in Russia but grew up in America. He was both a writer and a respected scientist. In 1950, he wrote *I, Robot*. The book told of a future in which humans and robots work together. During his long career, Asimov wrote more than four hundred books.

Ray Bradbury imagined a more troubling future. His stories were often about the dangers of technology. His novel *Fahrenheit 451* was published in 1953. In the chilling tale, television rules society. People are discouraged from thinking. Books, which are illegal, are promptly burned if found. The title *Fahrenheit 451* refers to the temperature at which paper burns. The book is still known today as a classic work of science fiction.

Arthur C. Clarke was a British author. He served in the Royal Air Force during World War II. Afterward, he studied the sciences in college. Clarke began writing science fiction books in the 1950s. But his most famous novel, *2001: A Space Odyssey*, was published in 1968.

LOOKING AHEAD

By the last months of 1959, Washington was abuzz with rumors. Many news reporters and political insiders believed that a young U.S senator from Massachusetts was planning to run for president in 1960. They were right. On January 2, 1960—the second day of the new decade—John F. Kennedy announced his candidacy. In July, he received the Democratic Party's nomination. In November, running against Republican Richard Nixon, Kennedy won the election.

Kennedy was the first president born in the twentieth century. At forty-three, he was also the youngest man elected to the nation's highest office. In his first speech as president, Kennedy told the country, "The torch has been passed to a new generation of Americans." Kennedy said that the United States would meet all the challenges presented by its enemies, especially the Soviet Union. But he also said that ways had to be found to lessen the chances of a nuclear war. He asked Americans to work for the good of their country, and he called on people everywhere to work for human freedom. With his youth, his energy, and his bold words, Kennedy inspired many people. He created a sense of optimism about the future.

Some great achievements would, in fact, occur during the 1960s. The civil rights movement would succeed in getting rid of laws that had made African Americans second-class citizens. Astronauts would walk on the moon and return safely to earth. Yet the 1960s would also be a time of conflict and turmoil—a situation exemplified by the assassination of President John F. Kennedy less than three years after he took office.

The election of John F. Kennedy in 1960 ushered in a new period of optimism and hope in the United States.

CHRONOLOGY

1950—In February, Senator Joseph McCarthy claims that many communist spies work in the U.S. State Department. North Korea invades South Korea in June. U.S. troops land at Inchon in September. China enters the Korean War in November.

1951—Julius and Ethel Rosenberg are convicted of spying in March. In April, President Truman removes General Douglas MacArthur from command in Korea. *I Love Lucy* debuts on CBS in October.

1952—The United States experiences an outbreak of polio. Jonas Salk develops a vaccine against the disease. Dwight D. Eisenhower is elected president in November.

1953—The Rosenbergs are executed in June. The Korean War ends in July. Ray Bradbury's *Fahrenheit 451* is published.

1954—The U.S. Senate condemns Joseph McCarthy for his reckless claims. The first successful organ transplant is performed.

1955—The Salk polio vaccine is first used widely. "Rock Around the Clock" becomes the first rock-and-roll hit. Rosa Parks is arrested for refusing to give up her bus seat in December. Her actions spur the civil rights movement.

1956—Tunisia gains independence from France in March. Elvis Presley begins his rise to stardom. The Suez crisis erupts in October. President Eisenhower is reelected in November.

1957—The Suez Canal reopens in March. Jack Kerouac's Beat novel *On the Road* is published. The Soviet Union's *Sputnik 1* orbits Earth in October.

1958—America's *Explorer 1* is launched in January. Fidel Castro leads the Cuban Revolution.

1959—Castro takes power in Cuba. Alaska and Hawaii become the forty-ninth and fiftieth states of the Union.

GLOSSARY

canal—A man-made waterway that allows ships to shorten their journey.

colony—A territory that is controlled by a distant nation.

communism—A type of political and economic system in which all citizens are supposed to share work and property equally.

crisis—An unstable situation; an emergency.

independence—The state of being free and self-sufficient.

lyrics—The words of a song.

melody—A song's tune.

orbit—The path of an object as it revolves around a planet or other body.

peninsula—A piece of land that juts out into a body of water.

population—The total number of people living in an area.

revolution—Sweeping change that leads to the overthrow of a government.

satellite—An orbiting object in space.

segregation—The practice of keeping people separate based on race or other differences.

superpower—An extremely powerful country, especially one that leads other countries.

transplant—The act of taking an organ from one body and putting it into another.

transportation—The business of moving people or goods.

truce—An agreement to stop fighting; a cease-fire.

FURTHER READING

Bobek, Milan, editor. *Decades of the Twentieth Century: The 1950s*. Pittsburgh, Pa.: Eldorado Ink, 2005.

Carey, Charles W., editor. *Living Through the Korean War*. San Diego, Calif.: Greenhaven Press, 2006.

Crompton, Samuel Willard. *Sputnik/Explorer I: The Race to Conquer Space*. New York: Chelsea House, 2007.

Edgers, Geoff. *Who Was Elvis Presley?* Des Moines, Iowa: Perfection Learning, 2007.

Fitzgerald, Brian. *McCarthyism: The Red Scare*. Mankato, Minn.: Compass Point Books, 2006.

Hansen, Sarah. *Dwight D. Eisenhower: Our Thirty-fourth President*. Mankato, Minn.: The Child's World, 2008.

Haugen, Brenda. *Douglas MacArthur: America's General*. Mankato, Minn.: Compass Point Books, 2006.

McLeese, Don. *Jonas Salk*. Vero Beach, Fla.: Rourke Publishing, 2006.

Parks, Rosa, and Jim Haskins. *Rosa Parks: My Story*. New York: Puffin Books, 1999.

INTERNET RESOURCES

<http://www.cnn.com/SPECIALS/cold.war/>
Learn more about the Cold War with this interactive site from CNN. It includes maps, videos, and games.

<http://www.fhwa.dot.gov/interstate/history.htm>
Study how America built the largest highway system in the world. This site from the U.S. Department of Transportation contains audio and video clips, plus much more.

<http://www.nasm.si.edu/exhibitions/gal114/gal114.htm>
Trace the origins of the Space Race. The Smithsonian National Air and Space Museum describes how the race to the moon first began.

Index

Nixon, Richard, 56
Nkrumah, Kwame, 31
North Korea, 7, 9–11, 16–17,
    20–23, 26–27, 32–33
nuclear weapons, 6, 24–25,
    27

On the Road (Kerouac), 34–35

Parks, Rosa, 38–39
polio, 36, 37
Presley, Elvis, 46–47

Red Scare, 12–13
    See also communism
Ridgway, Matthew, 27
rock and roll, 7, 46–47
Rosenberg, Ethel, 24–25
Rosenberg, Julius, 24–25

Salk, Jonas, 36, 37

Schirra, Walter H., 51
science fiction, 54–55
segregation, 7, 11, 38–39
Shepard, Alan B., Jr., 51
Slayton, Donald K., 51
South Korea, 7, 9–11, 16–17,
    20–23, 26–27, 32–33
Soviet Union, 6–7, 12, 24–25,
    53, 56
    and the Korean War, 9, 11, 26
    and the Space Race, 48–51
Space Race, 48–51
spies, 24–25
    See also Cold War
Sputnik satellites, 48–50
Suez Canal crisis, 42–45

technology
    computers, 5
    and medical advances,
    36–37

television, 5, 14–15
    See also entertainment
Truman, Harry S., 9, 10–11, 13
    fires Douglas MacArthur,
    26–27
2001: A Space Odyssey
    (Clarke), 55

United Nations (UN), 28–31,
    42, 45
    and the Korean War, 7,
    10–11, 17, 20, 22–23, 32
UNIVAC computer, 5

Vanguard 1 satellite, 50
Vietnam, 30, 31

Webb, Jack, 15
Whitney, Courtney, 17
World War II, 5–6, 9, 11, 18,
    23, 24

PICTURE CREDITS

Illustration credits: AP/Wide World Photos: 25 (top), 35, 37, 38; the Bridgeman Art Library: 1 (bottom left); courtesy Dwight D. Eisenhower Library: 32, 40 (bottom); Getty Images: 4, 14, 15 (bottom), 27 (bottom), 34, 46 (top); AFP/Getty Images: 43; National Geographic/Getty Images: 19 (top); Michael Ochs Archives/Getty Images: 47; Popperfoto/Getty Images: 42; Retrofile/Getty Images: 18; Time & Life Pictures/Getty Images: 19 (bottom), 24, 36, 39; Government Press Office, State of Israel: 44; © 2009 JupiterImages Corporation: 46 (bottom); image ST-C22-1-62 from the John F. Kennedy Presidential Library: 57; The Kobal Collection: 54; Allied Artists/The Kobal Collection: 55; 20th Century Fox/The Kobal Collection: 7 (bottom); Warner Bros./The Kobal Collection: 15 (top); Library of Congress: 1 (top), 5, 7 (top), 13 (bottom), 25 (bottom), 52; courtesy National Aeronautics and Space Administration: 48, 49, 50, 51; National Archives and Records Administration: 10, 11, 13 (top), 16, 17, 20, 21, 22, 27 (top), 30; private collection: 12; used under license from Shutterstock, Inc.: 6, 8, 28, 40 (top), 41, 53 (top); courtesy of Harry S. Truman Library: 26; Leo Stern, courtesy of Harry S. Truman Library: 9; UN Photo: 29, 31, 45, 53 (bottom); courtesy U.S. Air Force: 1 (bottom right), 23; U.S. Department of Defense: 33.

Cover photos: the Bridgeman Art Library (Elvis Presley); Library of Congress (desegregated classroom); courtesy U.S. Air Force (Korean jet conflict).